# Rhymes for our Times

'A poet's reflections of a year in Rochdale.'

Ian Aitchison

PreeTa Press Ltd

# Dedications

To Jacky Daly

**Acknowledgements**

To Tony Layton for the introduction

To Alan Barton for his photography
alanbartonphotographer@gmail.com

To the Rochdale Observer for publishing many of these poems and allowing me to respond each week to one of their weird and wonderful stories.

To Paul and Rita at Preeta Press.

Published in 2022 by

Preeta Press Ltd, Bolton, Greater Manchester

preetapress.com

All Rights Reserved

Copyright Ian Aitchison

Iansupervet@aol.com

ISBN: 9781919634432

Printed by ImprintDigital.com

The right of Ian Aitchison to be identified as the author of this work has been asserted by him in
accordance with Section 77 of the Copyright, Designs and Patents Act 1988.

This book is copyright. Subject to statutory exception and to provisions of relevant collective licensing agreements, no reproduction of any part may take place without the written consent of the author.

# Introduction

Ian has been a poet since I can remember since our times together at Kirkholt Junior School. Comical anecdotes and lyrics seemed to come naturally to him even at such an early age, so it wasn't a surprise he'd be drawn to the art (and science) of the limerick (whose nearest rhyme, according to punk poet John Cooper Clark, is *turmeric*).

As a boy, joker 'Chisna', as he was known, would regale us, and his teachers, with tall tales, before bursting out laughing, holding his belly as it shook, and pointing blindly to the source of mirth – usually one of us lot. One of his funniest came after Ian, then aged 13, emerged from an interview with the fearsome spidery Bill March, headmaster of the former Rochdale Boys Grammar, at that time transmogrifying into "Balderstone Senior High School". Ian had been quizzed about his A-level preferences. "Are you intending the Sciences or the Arts in Sixth Form, young man?" asked Bill March in his ancient black gown. Ian said: "Probably both, sir!" Obviously not the right answer, but it sounded funny to us.

Humour is still never far from Ian's thoughts when scripting his beautifully constructed limericks, an art he's been working on for decades. And what an excellent format he's developed in wryly commenting on the previous week's news in his weekly slot in the *Rochdale Observer*. Running for nearly two years, these poems cover such esteemed topics as cats up trees (where the 'pussy ran free'), nicking lawns as well as flagstones and fridge-freezers, pencil-less polling booths, changing the clocks, Valentine plans, putting the bins out and useless tossers (actually pancakes for tea).

Ian always sees the funny side: it's a charming trait in our PC times, and he has his readers either groaning or laughing out loud. But there's a brilliant, cunning side to his rhymes too, craftily constructed, with Zen-like precision. In a matter of just a few sentences, Ian's poetry takes us to the heart of Northern life with laughter and love in every line.

Tony Layton, founder and chairman of Words & Pictures, one of the UK's leading corporate communications companies and former journalist who trained with the Rochdale Observer (1978-81)

# Contents

| | |
|---|---|
| GRAB THIS CAT'S TALE! | 1 |
| FLOODING HELL! | 2 |
| UP YOURS! | 3 |
| WIND OF CHANGE | 3 |
| LAWN RAID IN HEYWOOD | 4 |
| STOCK SOLUTION | 6 |
| HIGH ART SKIPPED? | 7 |
| NO-SHOW WOE ON THE 464 | 8 |
| PENCIL IN POLL SAVINGS | 9 |
| SACK WARNING FOR COUNCIL | 10 |
| CLOCKED IT! | 12 |
| MIND THE ROAD, TOAD | 13 |
| DON YOUR DIRNDLS! | 14 |
| OBE FOR ROCHDALE POET? | 16 |
| VALENTINE BANQUET | 18 |
| ON THE PULL | 20 |
| I'VE BIN OUT LATE | 21 |
| BLEEPING HELL! | 22 |
| BAGGED IT! | 23 |
| IT'S CHRISTMAS! | 24 |
| NEED MORE INFORMATION TENANTS? THE FLOOR'S YOURS! | 26 |
| HAVE THE LAST LAUGH CATH! | 28 |
| USELESS TOSSER? | 30 |
| SWINGING CLUBS BACK AT RIVERSIDE | 32 |
| HARDENED CRIMINAL | 34 |
| DRY HUMOUR | 35 |
| HOTFOOT IT TO THE HOSPICE | 36 |
| FLAT SPAT | 38 |
| CHEF'S ON SONG AND PICKS UP GONG | 40 |
| SANTA'S SOON – MIDDLE OF JUNE | 42 |

| | |
|---|---|
| YOGA AND OUT | 43 |
| GET ON COURSE FOR TOWN HALL REVAMP | 44 |
| I SAY TOMATO … | 46 |
| WRITE ON, REV! | 48 |
| FORWARD THINKING | 49 |
| PRINCE ANDREW WARNED: IT MIGHT BE GOOD HIDING! | 50 |
| DOGS ON TRAMS? A MUTT POINT | 52 |
| SPOTTED AT BUS STATION – A BUS! | 54 |
| SENIOR MOMENTS | 56 |
| NO END TO MY TALENTS | 58 |

## GRAB THIS CAT'S TALE!

Last week we were tickled with laughter

Was ever a cat story dafter

A pussy ran free

Got stuck up a tree

And so did the owner soon after!

The rescue was soon underway

They called the RSPCA

And as you would do

The Fire Service too

Who scaled the tree without delay

But one thing they never foresaw

This job's what the police are trained for

If your cat can't be caught

Cos your reach is too short

You need the long arm of the law!

**FLOODING HELL!**

More storms were predicted – we knew it

Had we done enough to get through it?

We'd spared no expenses

On new flood defences

Come hell or high water we'd do it

But after a deluge all week

The barriers coped with the peak

If levels had been

As in 2015

We'd be up some unpleasant creek!

**UP YOURS!**

More fireworks – that's well out of line

And culprits need more than a fine

Most folks in their anger

Would give 'em a banger

Right up where the sun doesn't shine!


**WIND OF CHANGE**

We need to start backing the Greens

Foul gases let's cut by all means

Let's help to make sure

The atmosphere's pure

So, start cutting down on baked beans!

## LAWN RAID IN HEYWOOD

Some thieves are the cause of much mirth

When they nick stuff of so little worth

But blimey that's crass

To pinch someone's grass

And make off with a roll of fake turf!

The owners in Heywood just laughed

Half-inching their grass they thought daft

But then what a chore

To lay it once more

They knew they were in for some graft

A small strip of lawn may fetch nowt

Grass thieves will get greedy no doubt

And soon they will figure

They need to think bigger

So Crown Oil Arena watch out!

But pilferer didn't you see?

You've been caught on CCTV!

Now our boys in blue

Are coming for you

You may not have long running free!

The police will say: "Now look here sonny

This grass nicking lark isn't funny

And if you've made brass

From that roll of grass

We'll nick you for lawndering money!"

**STOCK SOLUTION**

It's sad to see St Mary's plight

Whose flagstones were half-inched at night

Culprits will be sought

And when they are caught

A stretch inside should serve them right


But some folks would not take this line

They'd say let our heritage shine

Don't lock them away

Put them on display

Those stocks at St Chads should do fine!

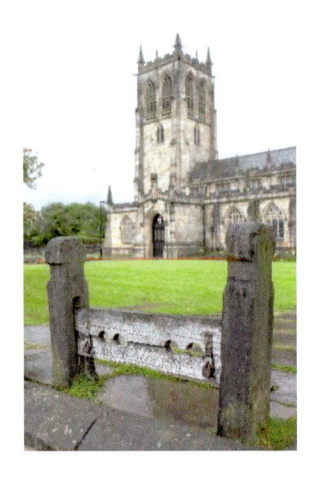

## HIGH ART SKIPPED?

A fridge-freezer perched on a cairn

Has certainly caused heads to turn

Artwork on display?

Or junk chucked away?

It seemed like we might never learn

But as I approached I thought – gosh!

This art is worth serious dosh

Cos I can swear blind

The work had been signed

No kidding – Hieronymus Bosch!

## NO-SHOW WOE ON THE 464

No wonder a chap got irate

When his bus for work twice turned up late

Rosso's 464

Had failed to show

So getting the sack was his fate!

Of course he was hardly elated

£5-40 he got compensated

You bet he's annoyed

He's now unemployed

And Rosso of course were berated

There's one thing I will say to Rosso

Concerning the 464 no-show

Folk won't get the sack

If you get back on track

But try to turn up before Godot!

## PENCIL IN POLL SAVINGS

Our local elections in May

Must run in a Covid-safe way

So do please take note

If you wish to vote

Then take your own pencil they say

Could this be some slick council ploy?

No sharpeners they'll need to employ

No pencils to buy

So they can't deny

Big savings they're going to enjoy

This should give the coffers a boost

With financial tweaking produced

But with money to spare

It only seems fair

Our council tax could be reduced!

## SACK WARNING FOR COUNCIL

I'm sure that we're all thrilled to bits

Now we can hire litter pick kits

But should we rent packs

Of vests, gloves and sacks

To make sure our streets aren't the pits?

But I've got a nice little ruse

A bundle of sacks I could use

There's kids on my street

Who love to compete

So sack races should be good news!

Just one pound to enter my race

Five quid to the kid in first place

If ten toe the line

Then five pounds is mine

A plan that I think's rather ace!

But now my plan's given away

I reckon wise folk won't delay

So council take heed

There'll be a stampede

Those sacks might just run out today!

## CLOCKED IT!

Tonight keep your timing on track

Change clocks before hitting the sack

And if you don't know

Which way they should go

Remember: Spring forward – Fall back!

## MIND THE ROAD, TOAD!

At twilight you'll see Toad Patrol

Preventing a grisly death toll

They're rescuing loads

Of frogs, newts and toads

Preserving wildlife is their goal

Down potholes some toads will not last

If they hide until speeders have passed

Some cars it is true

Will splatter a few

So Toad Patrol have to act fast

Now frogs' legs I don't think I've faced

But squashed toads should not go to waste

Just coat 'em in batter

Serve up on a platter

Cos toad in the hole's a great taste!

**DON YOUR DIRNDLS!**

Oktoberfest's wild celebrations

Is one of those beer-fuelled occasions

This weekend's the do

With Oompah band too

And Bavarian style decorations

The Champness Hall's hosting this hoot

Where you can get drunk as a newt

Most blokes will have chosen

To sport Lederhosen

Saves wringing out beer from your suit!

You'll certainly work up a thirst

Once you've munched on a few pretzels first

And German cuisine

Just has to be seen

There's traditional tasty Bratwurst!

But do get your fancy dress right

Make sure you're an outstanding sight

You're heading for fame

If you manage to claim

The prize for best dressed on the night!

If you need a dress you can twirl

To give table dancing a whirl

You'll need to impress

In Bavarian dress

So a dirndl's a must for a girl

Don't worry, the hosts won't compel it

But most fancy dress shops will sell it

I hate to announce it

But I can't pronounce it

And only the Germans can spell it!

## OBE FOR ROCHDALE POET?

I'm sure Tony Lloyd is excited

And all of us should be delighted

This outstanding guy

Has caught the Queen's eye

Fantastic to see Tony knighted!

But how is it that I was missed?

I'm not on the Queen's honours list!

She surely must know it

That I'm a class poet

Or have I been simply dismissed?

I'd never make mayor or MP

So probably no honours for me

But titles are many

So I'd accept any

Poet Laureate one day maybe!

I won't end up being a Sir

But readers will all be aware

She may honour me

With a new OBE

Observer Bard Extraordinaire!

## VALENTINE BANQUET

Have you made plans for your Valentine?

Are you sending chocolates or wine?

Are you keen on doing

Some intimate wooing

Or booking a restaurant to dine?

I should take the wife out one night

A meal out would be a delight

I'm not being funny

When it comes to money

The wife knows I'm pretty damn tight!

We all need to spend less that's true

Just look at the fuel bills now due

It only makes sense

To cut down expense

With council tax going up too!

But my cooking's quite hard to beat

I could knock up some special treat

I guess homemade nosh

Will save me some dosh

Then no need to go out to eat!


I'll make her a posh meal instead

Just need a tin opener and bread

It won't be a roast

Just baked beans on toast

And she can have breakfast in bed!

## ON THE PULL

My throbbing tooth's making me moan

And Covid has made it well known

It's best to get treated

Once you have completed

A dental appointment by phone

Would I be talked through an extraction?

I dreaded this next course of action

But I bit the bullet

Got ready to pull it

And braced for a painful reaction

But the dentist just wanted to say

How I could keep toothache at bay

I'd no need to try

Some tough DIY

So I've put my pliers away!

# I'VE BIN OUT LATE

It can't just be me in this town

Who puts bins out late like a clown

I'm slow off the mark

It's just gone pitch dark

So I can't tell the green from the brown!

**BLEEPING HELL!**

I don't use self-checkouts a lot

The queue behind think I'm a clot

I feel such an oaf

Rotating a loaf

When the bleeping bar code's hard to spot!

I leave the store after I pay

The door alarm bleeps on my way

"I'm not nicking owt!

Just frisk me!" I shout

"Could well be my thrill of the day!"

## BAGGED IT!

Advice for recycling's now rife

And we're told to get one bag for life

Well I did just so

Four decades ago

Still useful – and she's called the wife!

## IT'S CHRISTMAS!

As far as shops go I remember

When Christmas kicked off in November

But now there's a craze

For festive displays

Which seem to begin in September!

The shops tell us Christmas is here

(Which seems to be most of the year!)

We see festive food

Which gets us in the mood

And Christmas trees start to appear

The 'three for two' presents galore

Make me linger too long in one store

But it's sure time to stop

And get out of the shop

When 'Silent Night' comes round once more!

The girl at the till's sporting red

"That's a smart Christmas jumper!" I said

She's oozing good cheer

Dressed as a reindeer

Wobbly antlers perched high on her head

"Merry Christmas!" I say as I go

(I'm three weeks too soon – that I know)

I then hear her say:

"But it's three weeks away!"

And I say: "Well you started it though!"

## NEED MORE INFORMATION TENANTS? - THE FLOOR'S YOURS!

Some landlord has just made us roar

Has this ever happened before?

A renter was glad

They turned down this pad

As you had to lay your own floor!

If that's what a renter should do

Lay carpets and flooring brand new

It only seems right

When this comes to light

The landlord gets carpeted too!

If this is what some landlords do

Rent unfurnished houses to you

Might it be the case

They'd rent out a place

That's missing a window or two?

I don't mind if that's what they do

As long as their advert rings true

And outside the home

The name's clearly shown

I guess in this case: "DRAUGHTY VIEW"!

Suppose there's no roof on the place

Then renting would be a disgrace

A landlord could claim

The clue's in the name

Perhaps "HEAVENLY VIEW" in this case!

When a landlord's retirement is due

Their house name they'll need to renew

I guess they could aim

For a suitable name

"DUNRENTING" I reckon would do!

**HAVE THE LAST LAUGH CATH!**

Catherine's customer surely saw red

When they turned up and couldn't be fed

They saw the 'CLOSED' sign

And didn't half whine

Then scrawled a rude note to be read

This punter was rather irate

Bacon butties would just have to wait

Cath nipped off to grab

Her winter flu jab

So opened up two hours' late

There's customers like this I know

Who complain wherever they go

But a ready-made sticker

Would be a lot quicker

As scribbling a note's rather slow

In no time they'd then state their case

They'd have one to suit any place

No loo rolls at all?

They'd slap on the wall:

'NO LOO ROLLS – A TOTAL DISGRACE!'

And when there's no fuel to be had

Why waste time and scrawl on a pad?

Just stick up your own

Neat pre-printed moan

'NO PETROL – I'M PRETTY DAMN MAD!'

No need to start ranting and swear

Or moan that life just isn't fair

Most stickers I'd bet

Might contain this threat:

'I'M TAKING MY CUSTOM ELSEWHERE!'

So here's an idea for Cath

Stick up your own note for a laugh

Try this for a joke

Relax with a soak:

'NOT OPEN – I'M HAVING A BATH!'

**USELESS TOSSER?**

Shrove Tuesday means one thing to me

I'm sure that most readers agree

It's simply a matter

Of whipping up batter

And serving up pancakes for tea!

The wife knows I'm that kind of man

Who struggles to open a can

But shouldn't take long

And what could go wrong

With batter and one non-stick pan?

In no time she's getting damn cross

When cooking she's always the boss

She screams: "It's too brown

Just turn the heat down

And you need to start giving a toss!"

The wife's pancake skills are much slicker

But soon she yells out as we bicker:

"You really should turn 'em

Or you're gonna burn 'em

You just need to get flipping quicker!"

## SWINGING CLUBS BACK AT RIVERSIDE

If swinging clubs looks like your scene

Then Rochdale's the place if you're keen

Cos Puttstars is back

So do have a crack

That's golf – well, what else would I mean?

It's great family fun aimed for all

You'll laugh if you can't hit a ball

But some tricky putts

Might just drive you nuts

So book a slot – give them a call

I'm usually the butt of the jokes

And cause much amusement to folks

Cos after each thwack

The ball still rolls back

And that's after 25 strokes!

But once I've whacked off from the tee

I'm wary of my dodgy knee

So I've got a fear

Of carrying gear

So I take my caddy with me!


Now poets find English great fun

But plurals can leave me undone

It's just a wild guess

Where I place the 'S'

So, hole-in-ones or holes-in-one?

## HARDENED CRIMINAL

Shoplifting Viagra's bizarre

And shows how bold criminals are

Some bloke had a racket

He'd half-inch a packet

Then flog it to chaps in a bar

But some blokes I guess must be losers

Who buy dodgy stuff in their boozers

It's one big mistake

If tablets are fake

But beggars I guess can't be choosers!

Two tablets they say are OK

Just when you retire so they say

For me that's frustrating

I just can't stand waiting

Retirement's still five years away!

The packet I'd check carefully

And hope to spot some guarantee

But I'd be elated

If each packet stated

You've guessed: *'Extended Warranty!'*


## DRY HUMOUR

I'm glad when mid-January's here

Cos calendars aren't quite as dear

So take my advice

You'll get one half price

And miss just two weeks of the year!


When mid-January kicks off your year

Then Dry January's nothing to fear

Cos then when I choose

To abstain from booze

It's only two weeks without beer!

## HOTFOOT IT TO THE HOSPICE

Springhill Hospice are offering a treat

For those who can handle the heat

The task is to stroll

Through sizzling hot coal

But you need to walk in bare feet!

Do you have a burning desire

To tackle this ordeal by fire?

If you have a bash

And help to raise cash

Your guts many folk will admire

Now striding through glowing hot coals

Might suit just a few hardy souls

But please take my hint

It's best if you sprint

If you've got quite sensitive soles!

There's training thrown in with the price

In which you'll get expert advice

They'll run through the task

But I'd have to ask

Does that mean you do the walk twice?


Fund raisers who don't want to roast

Will zip across faster than most

But best not to race

And fall flat on your face

Or no doubt you're gonna be toast!

## FLAT SPAT

A refurb has whipped up a spat

So, Boris, who funded your flat?

Did I hear you say

Just £58K?

In Rochdale there's houses for that!

That figure's a crazy excess

No wonder you're in such a mess

You really could go for

A much cheaper sofa

I got one half price – DFS!

And if you need cupboards brand new

There's two things that you need to do

If folk start to nag

Just hide the price tag

And check them for skeletons too!

If you've John Lewis blinds in your office

Then some passers-by might just notice

But if you rip them out

You'll hear some folk shout:

*'It looks like it's curtains for Boris!'*

## CHEF'S ON SONG AND PICKS UP GONG

Milnrow Balti has gained great renown

So curry fanatics get down

The fare is exquisite

So make sure you visit

The 'Best Indian Restaurant' in town!

New diners I reckon will hurry

To visit these top Kings of Curry

But if isolating

It won't be frustrating

They'll deliver to you – so don't worry!

Bodrul Alom has sure made the grade

Fine culinary skills he's displayed

Top marks he's achieved

And so he's received

A superb 'Best Chef' accolade!

Now scooping the 'Best Indian' prize

Was just meat and drink to these guys

I might pop in too

Try their vindaloo

Although it brings tears to my eyes!

Just thought of a chap I once knew

Who twice a day scoffed vindaloo

It cost him some dosh

Not just for the nosh

But all the loo rolls he got through!

## SANTA'S SOON – MIDDLE OF JUNE!

Mecca Bingo were having a ball

With a grand festive catch-up for all

A June Christmas fling

Had seemed a great thing

With Santa Claus paying a call

So where did he park up his sleigh?

He must have been blocking the way

With Donner and Blitzen

And Dasher and Vixen

He'd surely need more than one bay

But he'd have been happy to see

In Rochdale he'd save on a fee

If he looked around

Then he would have found

There's three hours' parking for free!

But if he parked outside a bay

He might find a clamp on his sleigh

And then what a fuss

Getting home on the bus

The North Pole's a hell of a way!


## YOGA AND OUT

The wife's started yoga once more

Tweaked a groin as she stretched on the floor

It ain't gonna suit her

We tried Kama Sutra

She'd cramp when we got to page four!


(Not true actually! She'd cramp by page two – but that would ruin the rhyme!)

## GET ON COURSE FOR TOWN HALL REVAMP

Are you short of summat to do?

Can you spare the odd day or two?

The chance is now here

So please volunteer

The town hall revamp is now due

But note you'll be grafting for free

You certainly won't get a fee

But after your task

I guess if you ask

I'm sure you'll be offered some tea!

Now one thing you might find appealing

If you don't get that vertigo feeling

If working at height

Won't give you a fright

There's work to be done on the ceiling

Ceiling panels need delicate care

And the chance to restore them is rare

Some love it I've heard

But I'd be too scared

As scaffolding gives me a scare!

For this work there'll be a long queue

And I guess they'll select just a few

To prove you've the skill

And should fit the bill

I think this is what you should do:

Just say that you seem to recall

Your last work could brighten the hall

And when you sign in

Just write with a grin:

'Michelangelo – no job too small!'

## I SAY TOMATO …

So, some sociolinguists have found

There's four distinct dialects around

'Manc', 'Wigan' – and gosh!

There's one classed as 'posh'

But ours is a 'Lancashire' sound

In Oldham when they mention 'bus'

They usually rhyme it with 'fuzz'

But we just say 'bus'

And rhyme it with 'fuss'

So clearly they're not one of us!

Now really it's got to be tosh

To claim nearby boroughs talk 'posh'

It's not how they speak

That makes 'em unique

It's cos they are not short of dosh!

We'll probably agree that 'potato'

In all dialects should rhyme with 'Plato'

But oh how absurd

If you ever heard

The residents here say 'tomato'!

Now Wigan folk can't be mistook

You'll tell 'em from how they say 'book'

For us it's a book

Which just rhymes with 'luck'

But they always rhyme it with 'fluke'

As far as dogs go – what's the truth?

Doggy dialects? – Do we have proof?

We know sure enough

That our dogs say 'wuf'

But do dogs in Wigan say 'woof'?

## WRITE ON, REV!

The rebel Rev Coleman's been ace

And boldly he's stated his case

A message for all

He's chalked on the wall

At a Member of Parliament's place

This Rev is a staunch activist

On green policies he'll insist

His irate reaction

To climate inaction

By passers-by cannot be missed

Would this move the MP at all?

Would he for some new measures call?

Swift action we need

So MP take heed

Cos the writing is now on the wall!

## FORWARD THINKING

You'll know clocks go forward tonight

And most people should get this right

But this chap I know

Finds it a real chore

To be honest – he's not very bright

I said best to put your clock ahead

Last thing before going to bed

But he looked confused

And somewhat bemused

Then this cracked me up when he said:

'Before bed? – That's really not on!'

Cos BST's not quite begun

I jump up at night

And put my clock right

On Sunday – exactly at one!"

## PRINCE ANDREW WARNED: IT MIGHT BE GOOD HIDING!

The Duke of York really should hide

There's no way out now if he's lied

But he'd get no hassle

Locked in Windsor Castle

With ten thousand men by his side!

If they've got a drawbridge and moat

And access is only by boat

It might take a while

To seize him for trial

US judges you'd better take note!

So could the Prince be on the brink

Of facing a stretch in the clink?

Would he find it hell

Confined to a cell

And what the heck would the Queen think?

But prison would not be too hard

He'd yell as a Grenadier Guard:

"OK chaps come on

Now porridge is done

Let's march round the exercise yard!"

But if he was tried over here

He'd face British justice I fear

He might get short shrift

A trial would be swift

And punishment could be severe

He'd surely miss out on his leisure

If locked up for life for good measure

But oh how ironic

And wonderfully comic

If detained at Her Majesty's pleasure!

## DOGS ON TRAMS?  A MUTT POINT

At rush hour there's often a jam

When several folk board with a pram

Commuters I fear

Won't like the idea

Of dogs being brought on the tram

So will pooches travel for free?

Maybe – if they're sat on your knee

But if they must pay

The ticket I'd say

Should be a 'Day Rover' hee-hee!

At present it seems a big ask

To get folk to stick on a mask

For me it's just crazy

When people are lazy

It's not such a difficult task

Unlike people dogs are not fools

And they're great at following rules

They learn straight away

When told 'sit' or 'stay'

And don't need to spend time in schools!

So on the tram tannoy they'll play

A message for dogs which will say:

"Thanks for not barking

When you were embarking

And wearing a muzzle today!"

## SPOTTED AT BUS STATION – A BUS!

We stand here in all kinds of weather

Till we get to the end of our tether

No bus is in sight

Then what a delight

When three of them turn up together!

That did happen once I recall

But now they're just not on the ball

And I've heard folk say

They've waited all day

And no bus has turned up at all!

You'll know when a bus does appear

Not from the announcement you'll hear

But from the great sound

That ripples around

When all of the passengers cheer!

Now I've heard some pensioners say

A taxi back home's the best way

The taxis aren't free

But do guarantee

You'll get back home on the same day!

Last week I made this observation

There's a regular bus from the station

It leaves every minute

With not a soul in it

'NOT IN SERVICE' is its destination!

## SENIOR MOMENTS

My memory's started to crack

And a sense of direction I lack

If I'm leaving home

My dog has to come

As he always knows the way back

It's tough with incontinence too

And some things I can't always do

I always demand

The Gents is to hand

Oh sorry! – I just need the loo!

I'll drop off to sleep just for fun

After putting the frying pan on

I'm roused with a cough

Smoke alarm's just gone off

Good job I like bacon well done

I could win a fun run at last

I've often dropped out in the past

Now us OAPs

Might have dodgy knees

But mobility scooters are fast!

And having a bath is a chore

When I can't lift my foot off the floor

Must go to the gym

And get back in trim

Can't get my leg over no more!

# NO END TO MY TALENTS

I once knocked out limericks for fun

Now I'm senile that last line won't come

It ain't half a shock

When you get writer's block …